F O C U S   O N
Writing Composition 4

Ray Barker   Louis Fidge

	Classic fiction	Adaptation for TV or film	Range of genres	Classic poetry	Range of poetry	Classic drama	Autobiography/biography	Journalistic writing	Reports	Discussion texts	Formal writing	Explanations	Reference text	
FICTION							**NON-FICTION**							
	✓													
			✓							✓		✓		
			✓				✓							
	✓	✓	✓											
	✓					✓								
				✓	✓									
			✓				✓			✓		✓		
			✓				✓							
			✓				✓							
							✓	✓				✓		
	✓		✓											
	✓		✓											
	✓													
					✓									
								✓	✓			✓		
								✓	✓			✓		
									✓	✓				
	✓											✓		
								✓						
	✓		✓											
					✓									
							✓					✓		

2

Contents

Think ahead

Manny Rat is very definitely the villain in this story. What does he do that tells you this? Which words tell you he is not very nice? You – as the writer – can change all this.

The mouse and his child are a wind-up clockwork toy, who escape from a toyshop, only to find greater dangers on the road.

A large rat crept out of the shadows of the girders into the light of the overhead lamps, and stood up suddenly on his hind legs before the mouse and his child. He wore a greasy scrap of silk paisley tied with dirty string in the manner of a dressing gown, and he smelled of darkness, of stale and mouldy things, and garbage. He was there all at once and with a look of tenure, as if he had been waiting always just beyond their field of vision, and once let in would never go away. In the eerie blue glare he peered beadily at father and son, and his eyes, as passing headlights came and went, flashed blank and red like two round tiny ruby mirrors. His whiskers quivered as his face came closer; he bared his yellow teeth and smiled, and a paw shot out to strike the mouse and his child a rattling blow that knocked them flat.

"Time to be moving along now," said the rat. He set them on their feet, wound up the father, and guided them across the bridge and up the road towards the dump.

From *The Mouse and His Child* by Russell Hoban

Thinking back

1 Which word in the first sentence tells you how Manny Rat moves?
2 a) Where does he come from – the light or the shadows?
  b) Which makes him sound creepier?
3 a) What is he wearing?
  b) Do you find this very pleasant?
4 Write down the adjectives which the author has chosen to describe:
  a) the silk b) the string c) his smell.
5 a) What does Manny do to the mouse and his child?
  b) What does this prove about the kind of character he is?
6 Just before he does this, he smiles. How does this make the action even worse?
7 a) Where does he take them?
  b) Do you think this will be a pleasant place?
  c) Do you think this episode in the story is going to turn out happily or sadly?

Thinking about it

Take the description of Manny Rat and change it so that Manny does not seem to be a villain. (Use copymaster 1.)
- You will need to look at the adjectives you use to describe him. Adjectives also tell your reader the way you feel about the character, for example Russell Hoban could have used 'walked' to describe the movement of Manny, but he chose 'crept' because it makes the character seem creepy and secretive.
- You will also need to change the appearance of the character, for example what he wears.
- Finally, you should look at what the character does.

Thinking it through

1 Write your own portrait of an heroic character, such as Superwoman.
- What words would you use to describe: her appearance? the way she acts? the way she moves?
- What kind of actions does she perform? Why?
2 Now portray the same character as a villain.
- Use the same structure. Use different words and actions to change the way we think of her.

UNIT 2   Changing the Story – Retelling

Think ahead

This is an example of a 'parable' – a story told to teach a lesson or make a serious idea clearer. Why do you think parables are often found in religious writing? What do you think is the point of this story?

There was once a man who had two sons: and the younger said to his father, "Father, give me my share of the property". So he divided his estate between them.

A few days later the younger son turned the whole of his share into cash and left home for a distant country, where he squandered it in reckless living. He had spent it all, when a severe famine fell upon that country and he began to feel the pinch. So he went and attached himself to one of the local landowners, who sent him on to his farm to mind the pigs. He would have been glad to fill his belly with the pods that the pigs were eating; and no one gave him anything. Then he came to his senses and said, "How many of my father's paid servants have more food than they can eat, and here am I, starving to death! I will set off and go to my father, and say to him, 'Father, I have sinned, against God and against you; I am no longer fit to be called your son; treat me as one of your paid servants.'"

So he set out for his father's house. But while he was still a long way off his father saw him, and his heart went out to him. He ran to meet him, flung his arms around him, and kissed him. The son said, "Father, I have sinned, against God and against you; I am no longer fit to be called your son." But the father

said to his servants, "Quick! fetch a robe, my best one, and put
it on him; put a ring on his finger and shoes on his feet. Bring
the fatted calf and kill it, and let us have a feast to celebrate the
day. For this son of mine was dead and has come back to life; he
was lost and is found." And the festivities began.

Now the elder son was out on the farm; and on his way back,
as he approached the house, he heard music and dancing. He
called one of the servants and asked what it meant. The servant
told him, "Your brother has come home, and your father has
killed the fatted calf because he has him back safe and sound".
But he was angry and refused to go in. His father came out and
pleaded with him; but he retorted, "You know how I have slaved
for you all these years; I never once disobeyed your orders; and
you never gave me so much as a kid, for a feast with my friends.
But now that this son of yours turns up, after running through
your money with his women, you kill the fatted calf for him."

"My boy," said the father, "you are always with me, and
everything I have is yours. How could we help celebrating this
happy day? Your brother here was dead and has come back to
life, was lost and is found."

From *The New English Bible*, Luke 15:11 (The Prodigal Son)

Thinking back

1. a) How does the opening of the story tell you it is a traditional tale?
   b) How is it like the opening of a fairy tale?
2. a) Describe the younger son at the beginning of the story.
   b) How does he change in the story?
3. a) Describe how the father reacts when his son comes home.
   b) How would you have reacted?
4. a) Describe the older brother's reaction to his brother coming home.
   b) How would you have reacted?
5. Find details in the passage which show you:
   a) where the story is set   b) when the story is set.
6. Why do you think the story is more important than description in a parable?

Thinking about it

Write a modern version of this parable. Change the setting so it is a modern one, but you will still have to make the same important point.
- Introduce more characters, for example you could write scenes to show what happened when the prodigal son was away from home.
- Think about details which will make the farm and the city real places to your audience.
- Make the elder son a more interesting character. What is he like? What does he really think?
- Divide your story into sections to show the passing of time.

Thinking it through

Write a modern retelling of one of Aesop's fables. (See copymaster 2.)
- First decide on the point of the fable – what lesson is the writer trying to teach?
- Plan the steps you are going to follow to reach this ending.
- Fables are very short, so you will need to make the characters more interesting.
- Use description to make the setting more realistic.

UNIT 3   Changing the Story – Different Narrators

Think ahead

Does a story have to be told by only one narrator? How many narrators does this story have? Some people say that if you have more than one person telling you a story, then you cannot trust what they tell you. What do you feel about that?

In this book, the same story is told by two different people. Each short chapter is written like a diary, either by William or Neaera. They each give us their own story of how they decided to secretly release some giant turtles from the Zoo back into the sea.

William G

There are green turtles whose feeding grounds are along the coast of Brazil, and they swim 1400 miles to breed and lay their eggs on Ascension Island in the South Atlantic, half way to Africa. Ascension Island is only five miles long. No one knows how they find it. Two of the turtles in the Aquarium are green turtles, a large one and a small one. The sign said, "The Green Turtle, *Chelonia mydas*, is the source of turtle soup." I am the source of William G soup if it comes to that. Everyone is the source of his or her kind of soup. In a town as big as London that's a lot of soup walking about!

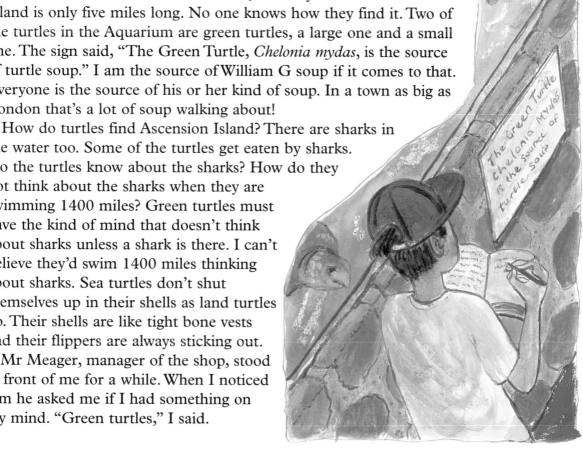

How do turtles find Ascension Island? There are sharks in the water too. Some of the turtles get eaten by sharks. Do the turtles know about the sharks? How do they not think about the sharks when they are swimming 1400 miles? Green turtles must have the kind of mind that doesn't think about sharks unless a shark is there. I can't believe they'd swim 1400 miles thinking about sharks. Sea turtles don't shut themselves up in their shells as land turtles do. Their shells are like tight bone vests and their flippers are always sticking out.

Mr Meager, manager of the shop, stood in front of me for a while. When I noticed him he asked me if I had something on my mind. "Green turtles," I said.

Neaera H

I had no intention of going to the Zoo but I went there. The penguins were yawping and honking. An Australian crane was performing a remarkable dance for his mate.

I stood in the darkness by the turtle tank for some time, not so much looking at the turtles as just being near them and waiting. A man in shirt-sleeves came out of a door marked PRIVATE and stood in front of one of the fish tanks as if checking something. He was obviously one of the keepers and he had an air of decency about him, as if he paid attention to the things that really need attention paid to them.

I rehearsed the question several times in my mind, then spoke to him. "Were any of the turtles full-grown when they were brought here?" I said.

"No," he said. "They were only little when they came here, no more than a pound or two. The big ones have been here twenty or thirty years."

"Full-grown turtles," I said, "How are they transported?"

From *Turtle Diary* by Russell Hoban

 Thinking back

1 William G writes more facts in his diary. What kind of person do you think he is?
2 Find examples in William's diary to prove he has a sense of humour.
3 Why do you think Neaera 'rehearsed' the question she asked the Zoo keeper?
4 Find evidence in Neaera's diary that proves she is planning to steal the turtles from the Zoo.
5 What do her questions tell you about what kind of person she is?
6 What idea is the same in both diaries, even though the narrators are different?

Thinking about it

Finish the story of the rescue and release of the turtles. Use the same idea of diary entries, one after the other.
- Think about each person's character and how it makes them act in a certain way, for example do they like/dislike something?
- Think about each person's different language and character. Does one person have more of a sense of humour than the other one?
- Only the basic facts are the same. Each person is writing his or her own little story.
- The coming together of these stories makes the piece of writing more interesting. Use copymaster 3 to help you plan your writing.

Thinking it through

Another interesting way of using different narrators in the same story is to get your characters to tell the same story through letters.
Tell the story of a rescue involving a fire, using letters. Each person involved in the rescue could write a letter to somebody else, describing what happened. In this way you will tell a story from the point of view of more than one character, such as a firefighter, a policeman, a nurse, the person being rescued or the mother of the person being rescued. Use the Stepping Stones to help you.

Stepping Stones to help you

- Do you want to write an official letter or an informal letter?
- The style should match the type of letter.
- Always put your address and the date.
- How will you begin? Dear Sir? Dear Mum? Hello there?
- How will you end it? Yours faithfully? Yours sincerely? Bye for now?
(Use copymaster P, Writing a Letter, to help you.)

UNIT 4   Planning your Writing

Think ahead

As a writer, you decide what you want your story to be about. Why do you think it is important to plan your story? What plan do you think was in this author's mind when he wrote this extract?

In this passage, Merlyn the magician changes the Wart into a fish so he can see what the world is like under water. The writer wants you to imagine what it must be like to change into something else, so he takes each stage, step by step. He has carefully planned out his story so you can imagine every tiny detail.

He found that he had tumbled off the draw-bridge, landing with a smack on his side in the water. He found the moat and the bridge had grown hundreds of times bigger. He knew that he was turning into a fish.

"Oh, Merlyn," cried the Wart. "Please come too."

"Just for this once," said a large and solemn tench beside his ear, "I will come. But in future you will have to go by yourself. Education is experience, and the essence of experience is self-reliance."

The Wart found it difficult to be a fish. It was no good trying to swim like a human being, for it made him go corkscrew and much too slowly. He did not know how to swim like a fish.

"Not like that," said the tench in ponderous tones. "Put your chin on your left shoulder and do jack-knives. Never mind about the fins to begin with."

The Wart's legs had fused together into his backbone and his feet and toes had become a tail fin. His arms had become two more fins – also of a delicate pinkish colour – and he had sprouted some more somewhere about his tummy. His head faced over his shoulder, so that when he bent in the middle his toes were moving towards his ear instead of towards his forehead. He was a beautiful olive-green colour with rather scratchy plate-armour all over him, and dark bands down his sides. He was not sure which were his sides and which were his back and front, but what now appeared to be his tummy had an attractive whitish colour, while his back was armed with a splendid great fin that could be erected for war and had spikes in it. He did jack-knives as the tench directed and found that he was swimming vertically downwards into the mud.

"Use your feet to turn left or right with," said the tench, "and spread those fins on your tummy to keep level."

The Wart found that he could keep more or less level by altering the inclination of his arm fins and the ones on his stomach. He swam feebly off, enjoying himself very much.

"Come back," said the tench solemnly. "You must learn to swim before you can dart."

The Wart turned to his tutor in a series of zig-zags and remarked, "I don't seem to keep quite straight."

"The trouble with you is that you don't swim from the shoulder. You swim as if you were a boy just bending at the hips. Try doing your jack-knives right from the neck downwards, and move your body exactly the same amount to the right as you are going to move it to the left. Put your back into it."

Wart gave two terrific kicks and vanished altogether in a clump of mare's tail several yards away.

"That's better," said the tench, now quite out of sight in the murky olive water, and the Wart backed himself out of his tangle with infinite trouble, by wriggling his arm fins. He undulated back towards the voice in one terrific shove, to show off.

"Good," said the tench, as they collided end to end, "but discretion is the better part of valour."

From *The Sword in the Stone* by T H White

 Thinking back

1   Genre: what type of story do you think this extract comes from? adventure? mystery? imaginary?
2   Setting: find details in the passage to show where and when the story takes place.
3   Characters: which characters has the author included in his plan?
4   Detail: what detail tells us that Wart had changed into something much smaller?
5   Planning: a) What does the extract start with? b) What does the author write about in the rest of the passage? c) How does the extract end?

Thinking about it

Finish the story. What adventures does Wart have under water, as a fish?
Draw out your plan, moving step by step through the story.
- How does the world under water appear to him?
- What would he see, hear, feel, smell?
- What would it be like to swim under water? Would it feel like flying?
- How big would the plants on the floor of the moat seem? Would he be able to see tiny things in the water that we would not?
- How would the other fish react to him?
- What dangers would there be under water?
- How would Merlyn help?
- Use copymaster 4 to help you.

 Thinking it through

Plan and write a story in which you are transformed into something very small or very large. Describe what the world looks like and feels like to you.
- Remember to go through the stages of your changes step by step so your reader can understand what the world might be like from your point of view.
- If you are big, everything will seem tiny. If you are small, everything will seem huge.

Stepping Stones to help you

- What type of story do you want to write? Science fiction? Historical? Something else?
- Where and when will the story be set?
- Who will be the main characters?
- How will you start?
- What will be the main events of your story?
- How will it end?
- What detail will you use to make this storyline really clear to your reader?
(Use copymaster A to help you.)

UNIT 5   Story into Playscript

Think ahead

This book was written as a story and later became a famous play. What is there in the action and in the characters that makes you think this would make a good play?

"Hullo, Mole!" said the Water Rat.

"Hullo, Rat!" said the Mole.

"Would you like to come over?" inquired the Rat presently. "Oh, it's all very well to talk," said the Mole, rather pettishly, he being new to a river and riverside life and its ways.

The Rat said nothing, but stooped and unfastened a rope and hauled on it; then lightly stepped into a little boat which the Mole had not observed. It was painted blue outside and white within, and was just the size for the two animals; and the Mole's whole heart went out to it at once, even though he did not yet fully understand its uses.

The Rat sculled smartly across and made fast. Then he held up his fore-paw as the Mole stepped gingerly down. "Lean on that!" he said. "Now then, step lively!" and the Mole to his surprise and rapture found himself actually seated in the stern of a real boat.

"This has been a wonderful day!" said he, as the Rat shoved off and took to the sculls again. "Do you know, I've never been in a boat before in all my life."

"What?" cried the Rat, open-mouthed: "Never been in a – you never – well, I – what have you been doing, then?"

"Is it so nice as all that?" asked the Mole shyly, though he was quite prepared to believe it as he leant back in his seat and surveyed the cushions, the oars, the rowlocks, and all the fascinating fittings, and felt the boat sway lightly under him.

"Nice? It's the *only* thing," said the Water Rat solemnly, as he leant forward for his stroke. "Believe me, my young friend, there is nothing – absolutely nothing – half so much worth doing as simply messing about in boats. Simply messing," he went on dreamily: "messing – about – in – boats; messing –"

"Look ahead, Rat!" cried the Mole suddenly.

It was too late. The boat struck the bank full tilt. The dreamer, the joyous oarsman, lay on his back at the bottom of the boat, his heels in the air.

"– about in boats – or with boats," the Rat went on composedly, picking himself up with a pleasant laugh. "In or out of 'em, it doesn't matter. Nothing seems really to matter, that's the charm of it."

From *The Wind in the Willows* by Kenneth Grahame

Thinking back

1 What are the names of the characters in this section of the story?
2 Find evidence to show where the characters are and what they are doing.
3 a) What sort of character is Rat?
  b) Find some words which describe him.
4 What does Rat like doing?
5 a) What sort of character is Mole?
  b) Find some words which describe him.
6 a) What happens at the end of the passage?
  b) Does the way Rat reacts surprise you or not? Give reasons.

Thinking about it

1 Write the passage as a 'playscript'. Use copymaster 5 to help you.
  Follow the Stepping Stones so that you include all the features.
  – Write down what the characters say.
  – Decide what happens in the passage and in what order.
  – Decide what stage directions you need so the actors can show you how
    the characters are feeling as well as what they are doing.
  – How will you give your audience the sense of location?
2 Write the next scene of the play. What happens when they are on the boat?
  Who else comes along?

Thinking it through

Use a 'ballad', for example 'Sir Patrick Spens' on page 18 or another story in
poem, and turn it into a playscript.
Use all the features described in the Stepping Stones.

Stepping Stones to help you

- Write the characters names on the left.
- Start a new line each time a new character speaks.
- Do not use speech marks.
- Do not use 'he said', 'she said', and so on.
- Use stage directions for the actions.
- Write the stage directions in brackets (or in italics if you have a word
  processor).
- Use prompts for actors in brackets.
(Use copymaster B.)

UNIT 6 Writing your own Poems

Think ahead

*When you write poems, it is best to follow a pattern. What kind of pattern can you
see in the ballad below? How many lines are there in each verse? Which lines rhyme
with each other? Why do you think people wrote ballads like this one hundreds of
years ago?*

The king sits in Dunfermline town
Drinking the blood-red wine:
"O where will I get a good sailor,
To sail this ship of mine?"

Up and spake an elder knight,
Sat at the king's right knee:
"Sir Patrick Spens is the best sailor
That ever sailed the sea."

The king has written a braid* letter   * long
And sealed it with his hand.
And sent it to Sir Patrick Spens
Who was walking on the strand*.   *beach

"To Noroway*, to Noroway,   *Norway
To Noroway o'er the foam;
The king's own daughter of Noroway,
"Tis thou must bring her home!"

The first line that Sir Patrick read
A loud, loud laugh laughed he:
The next line that Sir Patrick read
The tear blinded his ee*.   *eye

"O who is this has done this deed,
This ill deed unto me;
To send me out this time o' the year
To sail upon the sea?"

"Make haste, make haste, my merry men all,
Our good ship sails the morn."
"O say not so, my master dear,
For I fear a deadly storm."

"I saw the new moon yestere'en
With the old moon in her arm;
And if we go to sea master,
I fear we'll come to harm."

They had not sailed a league, a league,
A league but barely three,
When the sky grew dark, the wind blew loud,
And angry grew the sea.

The anchor broke, the topmast split,
'Twas such a deadly storm.
The waves came over the broken ship
Till all her sides were torn.

O long, long may the ladies sit
With their fans into their hand,
Or ere they see Sir Patrick Spens
Come sailing to the strand.

O long, long may the maidens stand
With their gold combs in their hair,
Before they'll see their own dear loves
Come home to greet them there.

O forty miles off Aberdeen
'Tis fifty fathoms deep.
And there lies good Sir Patrick Spens
With the Scots Lords at his feet.

From *Sir Patrick Spens* (Anon ballad)

Thinking back

1 Describe briefly what happens to Sir Patrick Spens.
2 Find evidence in the poem to show you where the poem is set and at what time in the past.
3 Sir Patrick agrees to fetch the King's daughter, even though he knows it is dangerous. What kind of person do you think he is as the hero of this ballad?
4 How many lines are there in each verse?
5 Which lines have: a) the most syllables? b) the fewest syllables?
6 Which lines rhyme in each verse?

 Thinking about it

Write two extra verses for this or another ballad, using its pattern as a model.
– You could write the verses describing the terrible storm at sea and how Sir Patrick Spens showed he was a hero.
– You could imagine you were the king when you hear the news of the shipwreck. How would you feel about this brave sailor dying?
– Think about how you can use some old-fashioned language to make it seem like the original ballad.
Use copymaster 6 for further ideas.

 Thinking it through

Ballads were often written about heroic deeds in the past. Write four verses for a new ballad about heroic deeds set in modern times, for example a lifeboat rescue or the landing of a spaceship.
– You could divide the story up as a class and each group could write their section. In this way you will finish with a very long poem.
– Come together at the end and read the entire poem.
– Do the parts of the story fit together well?
– Does anything not work? Why?
– Edit the long ballad until you have a ballad which really works.

Stepping Stones to help you

• Ballads are normally dramatic and must tell a story.
• The verses have four lines. The second and fourth lines of each verse rhyme.
• There are usually four strong beats in lines 1 and 3, and three strong beats in lines 2 and 4.
(Use copymaster C for more guidance.)

UNIT 7   Biography

Think ahead

Here, someone tells us about how Anne Frank first received her diary. It is from a biography. What is the difference between a biography and an autobiography?

Anne Frank woke at six o'clock in the morning on Friday June 12. She could hardly wait to get out of bed. That she was up so early was not surprising, since today was her thirteenth birthday.

It was wartime, 1942. Anne was living with her father, mother and sister, Margot, in a housing development in Amsterdam, the capital city of the Netherlands. The Netherlands had been occupied for two years by the Germans, who had launched a campaign of discrimination and persecution against the Jews. It was becoming increasingly difficult for Jews such as the Frank family to lead ordinary lives, but Anne was not thinking about that on her birthday.

The whole family gathered in the living room to unwrap Anne's presents.

Anne received many gifts that day, including books, a jigsaw puzzle, a brooch and candy. But her best present was one given by her parents that morning: a hard cover diary, bound in red and white checkered cloth. She had never had a diary before and was delighted with the gift. Anne had many friends, both boys and girls, but with them she talked only about everyday things. But now Anne's diary would be her very best friend, a friend she could trust with everything. She called her new friend 'Kitty'.

On the first page of her diary Anne wrote: "I hope I shall be able to confide in you completely, as I have never been able to do in anyone before, and I hope that you will be a great support and comfort to me. Anne Frank (June 12, 1942)"

On the inside of the cover she stuck a photograph of herself and wrote next to it: "Gorgeous photograph, isn't it!!!!"

Anne started writing to Kitty in her diary two days later, on Sunday June 14.

From Anne Frank: *Beyond the Diary* by Ruud van der Rol and Rian Verhoeven

Thinking back

1 Look at the first two paragraphs. In which tense is this biography written?
2 Is Anne writing about herself or is someone else writing about her?
3 Find evidence in the passage to show that the writer has given us a sense of time and of place.
4 Describe what kind of person you think Anne is from reading her diary entry here.
5 Do you think this passage is from the beginning or the end of the biography? Give your reasons.

Thinking about it

Imagine you are a famous writer. Someone has asked you to write a biography of someone you know. Choose a friend, or someone you know, as a subject. Write the first chapter, using the characteristics of biography you have discovered from this section.
- In rough, make some notes about this person. What have been the most important events in the person's life so far?
- Use your notes to help you write your biography. Remember that you must write it in the third person, for example: *The first memory Michaela had was when she was three. It was her birthday.*

Thinking it through

Choose a famous person, either alive today or from the past, for example Martin Luther King. Find out more about this person by carrying out research. Use reference books, CD Roms, and so on. Copymaster 7 will help you plan and make notes.
- What was his early life like?
- What did he believe in?
- What made him do what he did?
- How was he successful?
- What do people think of him today?
Write a short biography of the person and illustrate it.

UNIT 8   Autobiography

Think ahead

Here, Roald Dahl tells us about an episode in his childhood. It is from his autobiography. What is the difference between an autobiography and a biography?

My four friends and I had come across a loose floor-board at the back of the classroom, and when we prised it up with the blade of a pocket-knife, we discovered a big hollow space underneath. This, we decided, would be our secret hiding place for sweets and other small treasures such as conkers and monkey-nuts and birds' eggs. Every afternoon, when the last lesson was over, the five of us would wait until the classroom had emptied, then we would lift up the floor-board and examine our secret hoard, perhaps adding to it or taking something away.

One day, when we lifted it up, we found a dead mouse lying among our treasures. It was an exciting discovery. Thwaites took it out by its tail and waved it in front of our faces. "What shall we do with it?" he cried.

"It stinks!" someone shouted. "Throw it out of the window quick!"

"Hold on a tick," I said. "Don't throw it away."

Thwaites hesitated. They all looked at me.

When writing about oneself, one must strive to be truthful. Truth is more important than modesty. I must tell you, therefore, that it was I and I alone who had the idea for the great and daring Mouse Plot. We all have our moments of brilliance and glory, and this was mine.

"Why don't we," I said, "slip it into one of Mrs Pratchett's jars of sweets? Then when she puts her dirty hand in to grab a handful, she'll grab a stinky dead mouse instead."

The other four stared at me in wonder. Then, as the sheer genius of the plot began to sink in, they all started grinning. They slapped me on the back. They cheered me and danced around the classroom. "We'll do it today!" they cried. "We'll do it on the way home! You had the idea," they said to me, "so you can be the one to put the mouse in the jar."

Thwaites handed me the mouse. I put it into my trouser pocket. Then the five of us left the school, crossed the village green and headed for the sweet-shop. We were tremendously jazzed up. We felt like a gang of desperados setting out to rob a train or blow up the sheriff's office.

"Make sure you put it into a jar which is used often," somebody said.

"I'm putting it in the Gobstoppers," I said. "The Gobstopper jar is never behind the counter."

"I've got a penny," Thwaites said, "so I'll ask for one Sherbet Sucker and one Bootlace. And while she turns away to get them, you slip the mouse in quickly with the Gobstoppers."

Thus everything was arranged. We were strutting a little as we entered the shop. We were the victors now and Mrs Pratchett was the victim. She stood behind the counter, and her small malignant pig-eyes watched us suspiciously as we came forward.

"One Sherbet Sucker, please," Thwaites said to her, holding out his penny.

I kept to the rear of the group, and when I saw Mrs Pratchett turn her head away for a couple of seconds to fish a Sherbet Sucker out of the box, I lifted the heavy glass lid of the Gobstopper jar and dropped the mouse in. Then I replaced the lid as silently as possible. My heart was thumping like mad and my hands had gone all sweaty.

"And one Bootlace, please," I heard Thwaites saying. When I turned round, I saw Mrs Pratchett holding out the Bootlace in her filthy fingers.

"I don't want all the lot of you troopin' in 'ere if only one of you is buyin'," she screamed at us. "Now beat it! Go on, get out!"

As soon as we were outside, we broke into a run. "Did you do it?" they shouted at me.

"Of course I did!" I said.

"Well done you!" they cried. "What a super show!"

I felt like a hero. I was a hero. It was marvellous to be so popular.

From *Boy – Tales of Childhood* by Roald Dahl

Thinking back

1 Is this passage written in the past or the present tense?
2 Which pronoun does Roald Dahl use about himself all through the passage?
3 Is Roald Dahl writing about himself or is someone else writing about him?
4 a) Describe briefly the Mouse Plot.
   b) Do you find it funny or sad? Say why.
5 Why does Roald Dahl feel like a hero at the end of the passage?
6 Find three pieces of detail in the passage to show that Roald Dahl
   remembers what it was like to be a child.

 Thinking about it

Imagine you are Roald Dahl and write the next section of your autobiography
– the results of the Mouse Plot. What happens when you get found out?

 Thinking it through

Start writing a part of your own autobiography. Begin: *When I look back
on my childhood what I remember most is ...*
Make some notes on your life so far.
– What is your earliest memory?
– What was your first day at school like?
– Did you have any accidents/injuries when you were a child?
– Which festivals or feast days can you remember?
– What are your brothers and sisters like?
– Which is your happiest memory?
– Which is your saddest memory?
– Where have you lived?
Use copymaster 8 to help you plan your autobiography.

(Stepping Stones to help you)

• Use the first person – I – when talking about yourself.
• You do not have to include all details about your life – only the most
   interesting or important.
• Do not work through your life event by event.
• Illustrate your work with photographs.
• You do not have to start at the beginning of your life.
• Use speech in your writing to make it livelier.
(Use copymaster D for more guidance.)

UNIT 9   Different Ways of Writing about Characters

Think ahead

How much information can you get from this passage about Queen Elizabeth I? How do you feel about her? Do you admire her or do you feel sorry for her as an old lady?

Next came the Queen, in the sixty-fifth year of her age as we are told, very majestic; her face oblong, fair, but wrinkled; her eyes small, yet black and pleasant; her nose a little hooked; her lips narrow, and her teeth black (a defect the English seem subject to, from their too great use of sugar).

She had in her ears two pearls, with very rich drops. Her hair was of auburn colour, but false; upon her head she had a small crown. Her hands were slender, her fingers rather long, and her stature neither tall nor low. Her air was stately, her manner of speaking mild and obliging.

From a description of Elizabeth I by Paul Hentzner, 1590

Thinking back

1 Find a piece of evidence to show that the Queen is an old woman.
2 Why were her teeth black?
3 What does the author notice about: a) her earrings? b) her hair?
4 a) Would you say that the author likes or dislikes the Queen?
  b) Find words to prove this.

 Thinking about it

1 There are a great many facts in the description of Queen Elizabeth I.
Record the facts in a chart like this:

Age:	65
Face:	oblong

2 Imagine the Queen went missing. Use the information from your chart to
design a poster to help find her. Copymaster 9 will help you.

 Thinking it through

1 The author also shows that he admires the Queen. Copy and complete
this chart.

Description	Words which show he admires her
Way she walks Eyes Hands Way of behaving Her manner	majestic

2 Imagine an enemy of the Queen wanted to describe her using details in the
passage. Write this description in a letter to a foreign King. Which facts
would the enemy choose to create an opposite view? For example: *I saw
the Queen today. She was old and wrinkled.*

UNIT 10 Becoming a Journalist

Think ahead

This news article was published on the Internet. How can you tell that it aims to give you information as well as entertain you? What features make you realise that this is a piece of journalism?

April Fool!
By our humour correspondent, Ed Itorial

Every April 1st, millions of people all over the world will be made into fools. It's impossible to avoid April Fool's Day. It's the time for tricks. Maybe you will be caught out this time.

Anyone can be made into a fool on April 1st. It doesn't matter whether you are an important person or not on April 1st. Even whole countries have been tricked. Newspapers, television and radio all make a point of being foolish on this one day of the year. This has been a tradition in this country for centuries.

> *The first of April, some do say,*
> *Is set apart for All Fools' Day.*
> *But why the people call it so,*
> *Nor I, nor they themselves do know.*
> *But on this day are people sent*
> *On purpose of pure merriment.*
> Poor Robin's Almanac, 1790

All over the world

It's not just in this country that you have to be careful. The first of April is seen as a day of fun in many countries. In India, the last day of the Festival of Holi is March 31st. "This is traditionally celebrated by acts of mischief," an expert told us. If you live in France, someone who is fooled is called an "April fish"; in Scotland, April Fools' Day used to be traditionally two days long. Here, a fool is called an "April cuckoo".

However, if you live in Mexico or other countries in South America you would celebrate "Fools' Day" on December 28th. One guidebook tells us that it marks the time in the Christmas story when King Herod killed the innocent children. Once it was a sad time; now it is a time of good-natured trickery.

History

It seems that the idea of a day in spring when people behave madly goes back centuries. It marks the joy of coming out of the winter season.

In the Roman calendar, April 1st was the first day of spring. It used to be New Year's Day. Some historians say that when the Christians came to power, they wanted a day to make fun of all those who did not believe. This was April 1st.

Other experts of folklore believe it dates back to the Old French calendar which marked the beginning of spring on 25th March. The next eight days were for having fun.

The tradition has been taken all over the world by settlers and has even given us phrases in our language. For example "a fools' errand", was originally a joke search for something impossible on the day.

More fool you

One of the most famous television April Fool jokes took place in 1957. A serious programme called Panorama made a film about spaghetti growing on trees, and people believed it.

A few years ago, on a Saturday morning, a radio disc-jockey persuaded thousands of people that it was Friday – and they got up to go to work!

In 1998, a Portuguese sports reporter told listeners that their country had got through to the World Cup finals on a technicality. There were celebrations in the street.

On April 1st, 1998, we were told on the radio that scientists planned to cross a chicken and a chimpanzee to make a "chickpanzee".

It is easy to get your own back. One paper printed the story from a "reliable source", that in the Australian Olympic Games of 2000, there would be a new gold medal – for tuna-tossing.

And … how silly can you get? The Director of London Zoo told us: "We have to be very careful with phone calls on April 1st." Wouldn't you, if you received hundreds of calls for Ben Gwin, Sue Keeper and Ali Gater?'

So? Who's the April fool?

Thinking back

1 Write down the topic sentence in the first paragraph – the sentence that sums up the article.
2 How do the sub-headings in the article summarise what comes after them?
3 Find three examples of direct and reported speech in the article.
4 Why do you think articles such as this are written in such short paragraphs?
5 What is there in the first few lines to make you think the article is written as a joke?

Thinking about it

1 Make notes from the passage about April Fools' Day. Try to answer the questions:
 Why do people do it? When? Where? What is the reason for it?
2 Imagine you are a news reporter. Interview someone planning one of the pranks in the article. Write down what you think they would say, using details from your notes.
 – Write an introduction to explain the situation to your reader.
 – Set out the questions and answers like an interview.
 – Punctuate this correctly.
 – You could design it as an Internet page.

Thinking it through

1 Write an article for the Internet or a magazine for young people about an April Fools' Day prank which goes horribly wrong. Copymaster 10 will help you plan your article.
2 Interview others about tricks they have played on people and what has happened to them on April 1st. Write an article based on your interviews. Your articles could be collected together to make a class newspaper or magazine.

Stepping Stones to help you

- What kind of newspaper or magazine will it be?
- Who is the audience for the writing?
- What is the newspaper, magazine going to look like?
- What writing will go in the publication?
- How will the publication be printed?
- What will the front page be like?
(Use copymaster E.)

UNIT 11 Science Fiction as a Model

Think ahead

What will it be like to be a child at school in the future? Will schools have teachers, books, playgrounds? How does this passage give you a sense of what it might be like in the future?

Margie even wrote about it that night in her diary. On the page headed May 17, 2155, she wrote, 'Today Tommy found a real book!'

It was a very old book. Margie's grandfather once said that when he was a little boy *his* grandfather told him that there was a time when all stories were printed on paper.

They turned the pages, which were yellow and crinkly, and it was awfully funny to read words that stood still instead of moving the way they were supposed to – on a screen, you know. And then, when they turned back to the page before, it had the same words on it that it had when they read it the first time.

"Gee," said Tommy, "what a waste. When you're through with the book, you just throw it away, I guess. Our television screen must have had a million books on it and it's good for plenty more. I wouldn't throw it away."

"Same with mine," said Margie. She was eleven and hadn't seen as many telebooks as Tommy had. He was thirteen.

She said, "Where did you find it?"

"In my house." He pointed without looking, because he was busy reading. "In the attic."

"What's it about?"

"School."

Margie was scornful. "School? What's there to write about school? I hate school." Margie always hated school, but now she hated it more than ever. The mechanical teacher had been giving her test after test in geography and she had been doing worse and worse until her mother

had shaken her head sorrowfully and sent for the County Inspector.

He was a round little man with a red face and a whole box of tools with dials and wires. He smiled at her and gave her an apple, then took the teacher apart. Margie had hoped he wouldn't know how to put it together again, but he knew how all right and after an hour or so, there it was again, large and black and ugly with a big screen on which all the lessons were shown and the questions were asked. That wasn't so bad. The part she hated most was the slot where she had to put homework and test papers. She always had to write them out in a punch code they made her learn when she was six years old, and the mechanical teacher calculated the mark in no time.

The Inspector had smiled after he had finished and patted her head. He said to her mother, "It's not the little girl's fault, Mrs Jones. I think the geography sector was geared a little too quick. These things happen sometimes. I've slowed it up to an average ten-year level. Actually, the overall pattern of her progress is quite satisfactory." And he patted Margie's head again.

Margie was disappointed. She had been hoping they would take the teacher away altogether. They had once taken Tommy's teacher away for nearly a month because the history sector had blanked out completely.

So she said to Tommy, "Why would anyone write about school?"

Tommy looked at her with very superior eyes. "Because it's not our kind of school, stupid. This is the old kind of school that they had hundreds and hundreds of years ago." He added loftily, pronouncing the word carefully, "Centuries ago."

Margie was hurt. "Well, I don't know what kind of school they had all that time ago." She read the book over his shoulder for a while, then said, "Anyway, they had a teacher."

"Sure they had a teacher, but it wasn't a regular teacher. It was a man."

"A man? How could a man be a teacher?"

"Well, he just told the boys and girls things and gave them homework and asked them questions."

"A man isn't smart enough."

"Sure he is. My father knows as much as my teacher."

"He can't. A man can't know as much as a teacher."

"He knows almost as much I betcha."

Margie wasn't prepared to dispute that. She said, "I wouldn't want a strange man in my house to teach me."

Tommy screamed with laughter. "You don't know much, Margie. The teachers didn't live in the house. They had a special building and all the kids went there."

"And all the kids learned the same thing?"

"Sure, if they were the same age."

"But my mother says a teacher has to be adjusted to fit the mind of each boy and girl it teaches and that each kid has to be taught differently."

"Just the same, they didn't do it that way then. If you don't like it, you don't have to read the book."

"I didn't say I didn't like it," said Margie quickly. She wanted to read about those funny schools.

They weren't half finished when Margie's mother called, "Margie! School!"

Margie looked up. "Not yet, Mamma."

"Now," said Mrs Jones. "And it's probably time for Tommy, too."

Margie said to Tommy, "Can I read the book some more with you after school?"

"Maybe," he said, nonchalantly. He walked away whistling, the dusty old book tucked beneath his arm.

Margie went in to the school-room. It was right next to her bedroom, and the mechanical teacher was on and waiting for her. It was always on at the same time every day except Saturday and Sunday, because her Mother said little girls learned better if they learned at regular hours.

The screen was lit up, and it said: "Today's arithmetic lesson is on the addition of proper fractions. Please insert yesterday's homework in the proper slot."

Margie did so with a sigh. She was thinking about the old schools they had when grandfather's grandfather was a little boy. All the kids from the whole neighbourhood came, laughing and shouting in the schoolyard, sitting together in the schoolroom, going home together at the end of the day. They learned the same things so they could help one another on the homework and talk about it.

And the teachers were people.

The mechanical teacher was flashing on the screen: "When we add the fractions ½ and ¼ ..."

Margie was thinking about how the kids must have loved it in the old days. She was thinking about the fun they had.

'The Fun They Had' from *Earth is Room Enough* **by Isaac Asimov**

Thinking back

1   How do you know from the start that this is a science fiction story?
2   According to the author: a) how will children write in the future?
    b) how will they read?
3   What is different about the teachers that Margie and Tommy have?
4   a) Write down four things about a twentieth century school that Margie
       found surprising.
    b) Why was she surprised?
5   a) What things about your kind of school did Margie think was 'fun'?
    b) Would you agree with her?
6   How would you feel about being taught at Margie and Tommy's type
    of school?

Thinking about it

Write an account of Margie's school day. When each subject changes, allow
Margie to think about what 'fun' it might have been at your school.
–   You will need to think about how each subject would be taught by Margie's
    'mechanical' teacher, and what aspects of your present-day classroom would
    be 'fun' for her, for example sharing ideas in groups.
–   Use copymaster 11 to help you plan your ideas.

Thinking it through

Plan and write a science fiction story along the same lines as that in the unit.
–   First of all, make some notes on how you imagine some aspect of everyday
    life will be. For example, how will people travel in the future? What will
    people eat? What will they wear?
–   Imagine you are living in the future. Start in the same way as the story by
    finding an item or picture of something which makes you think about what
    it was like in the 'past' (how we live *today*).
–   Make some comparisons between your life (in the future) and life in the
    'past' (how we live *today*).
–   Your character can decide whether he/she thinks the science fiction future is
    better than the past.
Remember:
–   There is no need to have strange monsters in every science fiction story.
–   Look at the detail you need to use to convince your reader that the story is
    set in the future.
–   Most science fiction is trying to prove a point. What point is your story
    trying to make?

UNIT 12   Historical Fiction as a Model

Think ahead

How can you understand what it could have been like to be a child over four hundred years ago? Did they have boyfriends and girlfriends? How does this passage give you a sense of what it might have been like in the past?

This is the story of Nicholas, a fourteen-year-old boy who lived in the fifteenth century. He is the son of a wool merchant. He has been told of his arranged marriage with eleven-year-old Cecily. Here, he is writing a letter to her. Don't worry about some of the strange words like 'bearded sarplers'. They are old-fashioned words to do with the wool trade at the time.

Now that the excitement of the shearing was over life settled into a dull routine. Master Richard expected Nicholas to make up for lost time, and kept him long hours at his books. Very little else happened. The customary midsummer fair on St John's feast, judged by the standards of Newbury, seemed little more than a glorified market-day, but it served to break the monotony. Mistress Fetterlock, also, disturbed the peace by insisting that Nicholas must write a letter to Cecily. She knew of a messenger going that way and the chance must not be missed.

For hours Nicholas sat in misery at his father's counter, scratching his nose with the end of his quill. When he appealed to Master Richard for help, the priest replied with a smile that love letters were outside his province, and Nicholas should follow the guidance of his heart. But Nicholas's heart offered no suggestions. At last, in despair, he submitted to his mother's control, and wrote at her dictation a letter based on a scribe's collection of model letters. It was full of fine phrases and began by addressing Cecily as his 'Worshipful mistress and most sweet cousin' ('cousin', he was told, being a useful term which could cover any tie). It commended her piously to the care of the blessed saints, told her that he took no pleasure in life until he might be with her again, and that he was her true lover and humble servant.

He grinned to himself as he scattered sand over the ink, remembering Cecily up a tree, Cecily running away to track the Lombards, Cecily stamping her foot at them at the Fair. He sealed the letter with his father's seal – the merchant's mark so despised by Mistress Fetterlock – and then tried to forget it as quickly as possible.

The reply came in less than a fortnight, written in a round, childish hand. He had not known for certain that Cecily could write. After all, many girls were not taught anything but the domestic arts. But flowery as the letter was, he recognised a touch of the real Cecily about it. She called Nicholas her 'well-beloved Valentine' and told him that if only he were satisfied with her she would be 'the merriest maiden alive.' He laughed aloud at that. Of a truth he was very well satisfied.

But he had not yet finished with his letter-writing. One evening Giles took him aside.

"You are a scholar, young master," he began. "Could you make a letter for me to your worshipful father?"

Nicholas stared at him. "Has anything happened that is new?" he cried.

Giles shook his head. "It is just that Leach is sending away the wool for Calais. Since I found the bearded sarplers I have done all in my power to delay it. I have discovered reason after reason why it could not go, hoping that the master would come back. But now Leach will wait no longer. He is the packer and I cannot stop him. But I shall sleep better o' nights when your father has been told. I am no scholar, Master Nicholas, and I would not trust this matter to a scribe."

From *The Wool-Pack* by Cynthia Harnett

Thinking back

1 a) What are Nicholas and his nurse called?
 b) Why do you find this strange?
2 a) What did Nicholas write with?
 b) How did he dry the ink?
 c) How did he seal the letter?
 d) What would we use today?
3 Say what you find strange about the content of his letter to Cecily?
4 a) How did the letter get to Cecily?
 b) How is this different from today?
5 a) What does the passage tell you about how girls were educated in the fifteenth century?
 b) How is Cecily different?
6 Find examples in the passage of 'old-fashioned' language which give you the sense that this is a story about the past.

 Thinking about it

Finish the story in your own words. What happens about Cecily? What happens about the mysterious wool shipment that Leach wants to send, even though others want to delay it? What happens when Nicholas writes the letter to his father? Remember, Nicholas's father is away at the moment.
Remember:
– Look carefully at detail. They had girlfriends in the fifteenth century but Nicholas could not have telephoned her! What did people wear?
– Look at language. How did people speak to each other? Were they very polite? Did they use words we do not use now?
– How did people behave? Were girls allowed to speak? Were they educated?
– Do not slip into present day!

 Thinking it through

1 Imagine a boy or girl from another historical period is asked to write a letter to a boyfriend/girlfriend. It could be from Ancient Egypt, or from Victorian times. Write his/her story.
2 What details and language would make it sound accurate?
Use copymaster 12 to help you.

UNIT 13   Playing with Time

Think ahead

All stories have a beginning, a middle and an end. But do they have to be in that order? What happens to your story when you change that order? How does the author of this passage use time?

This story is about children of those Americans who bravely travelled across America in the nineteenth century in wagon trains in order to settle new lands. This passage describes how the wagon train organised itself to move on at the start of every day.

The day began like any other.

At four o'clock in the morning, when the rising sun stood like a red-glowing ball above the grey landscape, the guards fired off their rifles, as a sign that the hours of sleep were past. Women, men and children streamed out of every tent and wagon; the gently smouldering fires from the previous night were replenished with wood, and bluish-grey clouds from dozens of plumes of smoke began to float through the morning air. Bacon was fried, coffee was made by those who still had some. The families which could still cook maize mush for the children thought themselves lucky.

All this took place within the 'corral', that was to say inside the ring which had been made by driving the wagons into a circle and fastening them firmly to each other by means of the shafts and chains. This formed a strong barricade through which even the most vicious ox could not break, and in the event of an attack by the Sioux Indians it would be a bulwark that was not to be despised.

Outside the corral the cattle and horses cropped the sparse grass in a wide circle.

At five o'clock sixty men mounted their horses and rode out of the camp. They fanned out through the crowds of cattle until they reached the outskirts of the herd; once there, they encircled the herd and began to drive all the cattle before them. The trained animals knew what those cracking whips meant, and what was required of them, and moved slowly in the direction of the camp. There the drivers picked their teams of oxen out from the dense mass and led them into the corral, where the yoke was put upon them.

From six o'clock until seven, the camp was extra busy; breakfast was eaten, tents were struck, wagons were loaded, and the teams of draught oxen and mules were made ready to be harnessed to their respective wagons and carts. Everyone knew that whoever was not ready when the signal to start was blown at seven o'clock would be doomed for that day to travel in the dusty rear of the caravan.

There were sixty-eight vehicles. They were divided into seventeen columns, each consisting of four wagons and carts. Each column took it in turn to lead the way. The section that was at the head today would bring up the rear tomorrow, unless a driver had missed his place in the row through laziness or negligence, and had to travel behind by way of punishment.

It was ten minutes to seven.

There were gaps everywhere in the corral; the teams of oxen were being harnessed in front of the wagons, the chains clanked. The women and children had taken their places under the canvas covers. The guide was standing among his assistants at the head of the line, ready to mount his horse and show the way. A dozen young men who were not on duty that day formed another group. They were going out buffalo-hunting; they had good horses and were well armed, which was certainly necessary, for the hostile Sioux had driven the herds of buffalo away from the River Platte, so that the hunters would be forced to ride fifteen or twenty miles to reach them. As soon as the herdsmen were ready, they hurried to the rear of their herd, in order to drive them together and get them ready for today's march.

Seven o'clock.

From *Children on the Oregon Trail*
by A Rutgers van der Loeff

39

Thinking back

1 Write down four things that happened at four o'clock.
2 What happened at five o'clock?
3 Why was the camp extra busy from six o'clock to seven o'clock?
4 How many hours in total does the author cover in this passage?
5 a) Why do you think it was so important for the people in the wagon train to be so organised about time?
   b) What would have happened if they had not been so organised?
6 When the passing of time is described in its correct order, it is called 'chronological order'. Is this passage written in chronological order? Give your reasons.

 Thinking about it

Tell the story of a day in your life in the same way as in the passage. Begin:
The day started like any other …
– Move through three or four hours using the same plan. You will be writing in chronological order.

 Thinking it through

1 Use the events in a story from four o'clock to seven o'clock, but play about with time. Use copymaster 13 to help you.
2 You can use 'flashback' to tell the story of an exciting day on the wagon train, ending with a meeting with the Sioux Indians.
3 Write your own story using flashback. For example, if you wrote about the Titanic disaster, you could start with a man fighting through water to get onto the deck. After describing this, he could go back in time: *I had not expected this when I climbed out of bed this morning …*

Stepping Stones to help you

• Introduce your account with a general statement. Do not just start with the first event.
• Think of words other than 'and' and 'then' to connect paragraphs, for example 'first', 'next', 'eventually', and so on.
• Try to begin each paragraph differently.
• Use details to make each paragraph different.
(Refer also to copymaster F, for more guidance.)

UNIT 14   Writing a Parody

Think ahead

When you 'parody' something you take something well known and make fun of the language or style to make people laugh. Which of excerpts A to F is the original, serious poem, and which is the parody by Lewis Carroll? What makes the parody funny?

Lewis Carroll wrote the famous 'nonsense' books about Alice over a hundred years ago. In them he wrote parodies – he made fun of many of the serious poems of the times. Here are some of these poems and his parodies of them.

A Twinkle, twinkle, little star, How I wonder what you are! Up above the world so high, Like a diamond in the sky.	**B** Twinkle, twinkle, little bat! How I wonder what you're at! Up above the world you fly, Like a tea tray in the sky.

C Speak roughly to your little boy,
And beat him when he sneezes;
He only does it to annoy,
Because he knows it teases.

D Speak gently to the little child!
Its love be sure to gain;
Teach it in accents soft and mild;
It may not long remain.

E "You are old, Father William," the young man cried,
"And pleasures with youth pass away;
And yet you lament not* the days that are gone,
Now tell me the reason I pray."
　　　　*are not sad about

F "You are old," said the youth, "one would hardly suppose
That your eye was as steady as ever;
Yet you balanced an eel on the end of your nose –
What made you so awfully clever?"

Parodies from *Alice Through the Looking Glass* and *Alice in Wonderland* by Lewis Carroll

Thinking back

1 Copy and complete the chart. Decide which poems are the parodies and say why.

Poem	Parody	How I know
A	No	Quite serious. Not funny.
B	Yes	Talks about a bat flying like a tea tray – funny.

2 What serious things does Lewis Carroll change to jokes in his poems?
3 Does he ever change the form of the poem – the rhyme? the pattern of the verses?

Thinking about it

1 Write another verse for any of the Lewis Carroll parodies.
   – Look carefully at the subject of the serious poem he is making fun of. Decide on just one idea and write a comic version of that.
   – How does he make the serious things ridiculous?
   – What parts of the original poem does he copy?
   – What parts does he change?
2 See copymaster 14 to understand the pattern of the poem and to enjoy other verses.

Thinking it through

Take a well-known nursery rhyme, or even a pop song, and produce your own parody. For example:

Mary had a little lamb,
It was stupid, we all knew,
It followed her across the road,
And now it's mutton stew!

To do this you will have to look carefully at the original.
– How many lines in a verse?
– How does it rhyme?
– Does it use a particular pattern?
– Does it use a particular kind of language?
– How will you make fun of the idea in the original? For example,
   Little Bo Peep has lost her car
   Because it has been towed away by the traffic police?

43

UNIT 15 Constructing Effective Arguments

Think ahead

If you write an argument, does it mean that you have to have strong feelings about something? Should an argument contain both sides of the story? What does it mean when you only give your reader one side of the argument?

Smoking

A HOW MUCH SMOKING COSTS THE HEALTH SERVICE

Thousands of hospital beds are occupied each day by patients with smoking-related diseases, and one and a half million beds are used unnecessarily each year. This costs the National Health Service well over £100,000 per year for England and Wales.

B ILL HEALTH

Smoking is the greatest cause of ill health and premature death in England. Smokers are at greater risk of illness and early death compared to non-smokers. Smoking-related diseases include heart disease, lung cancer, throat cancer, breathing difficulties, ulcers. Smoking can also increase the severity of everyday complaints, such as coughing, sneezing and shortness of breath when running or playing sports.

Information taken from the Health Education Authority

C A CIGARETTE PRODUCES TWO KINDS OF CIGARETTE SMOKE

Roughly 75% of the smoke from a lit cigarette goes straight out into the air as sidestream smoke. The smoker inhales the remaining 25% as mainstream smoke, and breathes half of this out again. In total, 85–90% of cigarette smoke gets into the air which others breathe.

The Smoker

The smoker inhales mainstream smoke which contains a treacly tar (which irritates the lungs and can cause cancer), carbon monoxide (which starves the body of oxygen and may lead to heart attacks) and nicotine (a very addictive poison) plus a variety of other gases and poisons.

The passive Smoker

The passive smoker breathes in sidestream smoke diluted in the air. This is unfiltered smoke and contains higher concentrations of the poisonous chemicals and gases than mainstream smoke. It contains twice as much nicotine, 3 times as much tar, 5 times as much carbon monoxide, 50 times as much cancer causing chemicals.

 Thinking back

1. a) Write down two pieces of evidence the author uses to argue his case in A.
   b) What do you notice about this evidence?
2. Where do you think the author might have found this information?
3. Find a piece of evidence that the author uses to argue his case in B.
4. In C, apart from using words, what else does the author use to argue his case?
5. Which of the three examples uses technical language to convince you about the argument?
6. Is this kind of language easy or difficult to understand?

Thinking about it

Write an argument: 'Smoking costs us too much. It should be banned.'
Read A and B. In a chart, write the most important points. (See copymaster 15.)

Arguments for	Arguments against
beds used in hospitals	

- Write your own arguments against these points, for example 'keeps nurses in work'.
- When you have completed your chart, write out your argument in a paragraph.
- Use words such as 'therefore' and 'however' to help your argument.
- Use the Stepping Stones to help you.

 Thinking it through

Read the information in C about passive smoking. Write an argument against this. Write a letter to the Health Authority.
- Plan your argument in rough first. Use copymaster 15 to help you.

Stepping Stones to help you

- State what *you* believe at the beginning.
- Research the facts.
- Do not state your opinion as if it were a fact.
- Plan your points so that you reach a conclusion.
- Do not show that you are prejudiced.
- Give both sides of the argument.
- Back up your argument with examples.
- Use argument words.

(Look at copymaster G.)

UNIT 16   Reporting a Controversial Issue

Think ahead

Food and what you are allowed to eat in school is a controversial issue. We all have our own views on the subject. Do you sympathise with the views in these passages? What details help you to see both sides of the argument?

A WHO SHOULD DECIDE WHAT YOU EAT FOR LUNCH IN SCHOOL?

Children's eating habits in school.
Research findings for the Parents' Committee.

1 In our survey in local schools, half the children ate chips at lunchtime.

2 Doctors tell us that a high fat content in food is unhealthy. Children who eat a large amount of fatty food, such as chips, may become unhealthy in later life and suffer from heart disease.

3 School dinner supervisors told us that many children would not stop to buy a school meal if chips were not on the menu.

4 Chips are often the cheapest food on the menu. Some children said they ate chips to save money. They did not think about health.

5 Children who were trying to lose weight, often missed lunch altogether. They just had a fizzy drink. They knew chips were fattening.

6 Health education is not being successful in school. We saw children eating chips with their salad.

7 Children need more information about what is in their food and how it can influence their health.

8 Much more should happen in school to tell children about the dangers of their diet for later in their lives.

9 Food shops in school do not help. The crisps and snack foods they sell contain up to 70% fat.

B

Chips, burgers, biscuits and beans

"Take a piece of margarine, lots of lard and white flour. Mix it all up with water. Cook in an oven. Add some jam. Children love it!"

Presenters of the new TV cookery programme recommend this recipe! Children love these biscuits but are they doing them any good?

Bad eating habits

Teachers say, "No." They say this is the worst kind of food to be giving children in school and are trying to ban the biscuits from canteens. Such food, they say, is encouraging bad eating habits. Rather than selling these biscuits, canteens should be selling fresh fruit and salads. The biscuits are full of fat and contain no fibre which is essential to diet.

Fast food changes

Schools have moved towards 'fast food' for lunchtime. Traditional meals have gone. In their place are chips, burgers, beans and biscuits. They are cheaper to produce. They use fewer staff. But doctors say these foods could eventually lead to high blood-pressure and heart disease later in life.

"We could make no worst diet for our children than these biscuits," said the education chief this week. "Canteens need to become aware of what healthy food is."

The Head of a local school told us that junk food needed to disappear from school, but this would be difficult. "Give children money to spend in the canteen and they will buy chips. I can't imagine why."

Thinking back

1 How can you tell by the way it is set out that the report in A is in note form?
2 Why do you think the Parents' Committee might have carried out this research?
3 What use might they make of the findings in their school?
4 Does the writer in B make the recipe for biscuits sound tasty or nasty? Why?
5 Why does the newspaper article use quotations? How do they help the person's argument?
6 For whom do you think this article has been written?

Thinking about it

1 Before you write a report, you need to gather the relevant information.
Draw and complete a chart to help you summarise the views of the writer
in **A**.

Against the subject	Reason
Chips are unhealthy	High in fat Can cause heart disease later

2 Write the information from your chart as a report. Use copymaster 16 to
help plan and structure your report.

Thinking it through

1 Make a chart to help you think of opposite views (from the ones in these
passages) about food in schools.

For the subject	Against the subject
Too much fat content Chips should be banned	Some fat is good for you We should be able to choose what we eat

2 Write a magazine article. Use the information in this unit and your notes on
the opposite views, giving a young person's view on diet in schools.
   – Use figures and details from the passages to back up your arguments.
   – Research some more facts.
   – Do not write just your personal view.
   – Draft your report and check you are using the correct style.
   – Produce a final version. Find and use any pictures which might make the
subject and its issues clearer for your reader.

Stepping Stones to help you

Reports describe or classify the ways things are.
- They should have an opening statement making the subject of the report
clear.
- They should describe: what people think, the evidence for and against, uses,
reasons and comparisons.
- They should try to give different points of view, even if you really agree with
one another.
- Reports are usually written in the present tense.
(Use copymaster H for handy hints.)

UNIT 17 Filling in Forms

Think ahead

Sometimes, English can be very 'formal', especially on official documents such as forms. How easy is it to understand this formal language? Why do you think people use this language on forms?

Tracy needs extra pocket money. When she sees this advertisement she is very excited. Poor Tracy then receives the official application form …

WANTED
Young person for paper round.
Must be responsible.
Preferably have own bike.
Apply by letter to Smith's Newsagents.
Application form only.

Dear Mr Smith,
    My name is Tracy Black and
I would like to deliver your papers
for you.
    I am a very responsible person
and have my own bike.
    Please send me an application form
for the job.
    Yours sincerely,

Tracy

CONFIDENTIAL
Application for employment
(use block capitals throughout)

Surname of applicant

Forenames

Current address

Telephone number

Nationality

Date of birth   Age   Marital status

Do you own a bike? Y/N

National Insurance Number

Height   Weight

Do you have any physical disabilities that could affect this application? Y/N

Position applied for

Pay expected

Have you previously worked for us? Y/N

On what date would you be available for work?

Have you any skills, experience or qualifications that would make you especially suitable for the job?

Names and addresses of two people who can be contacted about you.

Signed by parent/guardian:

Date:

Thinking back

1 Why is the application form confidential?
2 a) What are 'block capitals'?
  b) Why do you think Tracy is asked to complete the form in block capitals?
3 What are 'forenames'? Check in a dictionary.
4 Which questions on the application form show that it is not meant for schoolchildren?
5 What skills or experience do you think would be good for this job?
6 Why is it important for the form to be signed by a parent or guardian?
7 Why do you think people have to fill out application forms when they apply for a job?

Thinking about it

1 Re-write the application form in simple language, then complete it as if you are Tracy. Use copymaster 17 to help you.
  Use a dictionary to check on some of the words if you do not understand them.
2 Design and complete another application form, for example for joining a club. Use the following headings to help you:
  – Personal details;
  – Previous experience;
  – Hobbies;
  – Guardian's agreement.

Thinking it through

You are a witness to a car accident and are sent an accident report form to complete.
Design and complete the form.
– What information would you need to give about yourself?
– What information would you need to give about what you had seen?
– What might you be asked about what you thought?
– How can you avoid using official sounding language?
– Will you need to include diagrams?

UNIT 18   Writing Back-cover Blurb

Think ahead

Why do publishers write so much on the back of a book cover?
How important is 'back-cover blurb' in making you want to read the book?
Which of these back-cover blurbs would make you want to read the book? Why?

A

From the safety of the toyshop to the slavery in the dump and escape through wood and meadow; through war between armies of shrews, through a first-night disaster with Crow's travelling players, through Muskrat's horrendous exercise in pure science and an encounter with a deep-thinking snapping turtle and the Last Visible Dog at the bottom of a pond; all the way to the final battle for the territory the clockwork mouse and his child endured whatever came their way in their quest for the beautiful dolls' house they once had known. And always on their track, determined to destroy them, was Manny Rat.

... *The Mouse and his Child* is more than a spellbinder. It keeps you spellbound in the sense that you sit on and read, but it has much to offer besides its galloping adventure, danger, and suspense. It has mystery, and jokes, and a sense of the almost awesome nature of happiness ...

From *The Mouse and His Child* by **Russell Hoban**

B

The diary of Anne Frank has deeply affected the millions who have read it since it was discovered and published. Now Anne herself, as a normal girl growing up, is portrayed in this moving account, with photographs of her life with her family.

In over one hundred pictures, many never before published, Anne's life before she was forced into hiding is uncovered. *Anne Frank: Beyond the Diary* captures the childhood of almost any girl we might know, one with a lively personality, friends, and family. We can imagine her hopes, her dreams. Photographs and excerpts from Anne's diaries expose the worsening political situation and oppressive conditions that marked the last years of her life. Finally, the testimony of the people who last saw Anne and her sister Margot alive reveals the tragedy that followed.

"A superb exploration of the particular and the universal meanings of a seminal work."
– *Publishers Weekly*, starred review

Winner of the Christopher Award
ALA Notable Book
A YALSA Best Book for Young Adults
Mildred L. Batchelder Honor Book

From *Anne Frank: Beyond the Diary* by Ruud van der Rol and Rian Verhoeven

Thinking back

1 a) In A, how many characters are mentioned in the 'blurb'?
   b) How many different settings are mentioned? How does this make the story seem more exciting?
2 a) The back-cover blurb mentions words such as 'war', 'battle' and 'determined to destroy'. What kind of story do you think A will be?
   b) What makes you think it will have a happy ending?
3 Write three things the reviewer likes about the story.

Thinking back (continued)

4 In B, the blurb mentions 'pictures' and 'photographs'.
   a) Why do you think these are important in a biography?
   b) Would this make you want to read the book more?
5 a) How many awards has the book won?
   b) Why do you think the publisher mentions these?

Thinking about it

Design your own book cover for a favourite book. Use copymaster 18 to help you. Write the blurb for the back cover. Include some of these ideas.
- direct quotations from the book;
- quotations from a reviewer;
- a quotation from the opening to get readers interested;
- questions to get readers interested;
- details about the author;
- other books in the series or that the author has written;
- any prizes the book has won.

Thinking it through

Imagine you are starting a class book club.
- Design a 'reading passport' so people can record the books they have read and what they think of them.
- Design a page called 'Three great titles not to be missed' for your book club brochure. Write back-cover blurbs for your three favourite books.

Stepping Stones to help you

- Collect 'blurbs' and analyse their features.
- Do they have: quotations from the book? information about the author? information about other books he/she has written? information about any awards the book may have won?
- Who is your blurb aimed at? Children? Adults?
- Does the blurb contain what the reader wants to know?
- Does the blurb tell the whole story or give too much away?
- Does the blurb make you want to read the book?

UNIT 19 Different Ways of Writing Book Reviews

Think ahead

Why do you think it is important to recommend your favourite books to someone else? What features of the book is it most important to write about? How do these children make their reviews lively?

A

Book Review

Title: The Witches
Author: Roald Dahl
Illustrated by Quentin Blake
Published by the Penguin Group
First published by Jonathan Cape in 1983

About the book

This book is very exciting and is about a boy called Samuel. He was born in London but his parents were Norwegian. His parents died in Norway in a car accident.

He survived but had a head injury. When he got better he went to live with his grandmother in Norway. She was quite old and fat and smoked cigars.

One evening she started to tell Samuel about witches. She said she knew all about them. Now Samuel did not quite believe his grandmother so he kept on asking, 'Is it true?' and the answer he always got back was, 'Yes. How many times have I got to tell you!'

Anyway, they all went to live in an expensive hotel by the sea. There were lots of witches in disguise there. They were having a meeting. One of these was the Grand High Witch.

The Grand High Witch wore a mask because underneath she looked like a spoilt rat with front teeth sticking out. She also had a nose sharper than a pen.

The witches planned to take over the hotel. The Grand High Witch came up with a plan to turn human beings into mice ...

Find out about the rest of the story.

star rating
* * * *
magnificent

Witch's mask

By Farhana Chowdhury

B

Certificate
Awarded to

Hector the Rat
This author is Tony Wilkinson

I chose this book because Hector is smart. He is a rat who reads a lot, like me. In the story some pink rats try to gang up on Hector. But he outsmarts them. He has to find out that humans are not all bad. His human friend saves his life. The story is also funny in parts.

I give this certificate to Tony Wilkinson

Signed by Shema Begum

Thinking back

1 a) Which of these reviews did you look at first?
  b) What made you look at them? the pictures? fewer words?
2 Which review gives you more information about the story?
3 What information is in A that is not in B? Copy and complete this chart.

In A	In B	Useful information?
Publisher and illustrator	Publisher not mentioned	Yes. You can find it in a shop.

Thinking about it

1 Design and write a certificate to award to your favourite book.
  – Explain why you chose the book:
    exciting story? good characters? funny? something else?
  – Give examples from the book. Remember, you have to prove to someone else that the book is as good as you say it is.
2 Write a more formal book review. Use copymaster 19 to help you plan this.

Thinking it through

Here are some other ideas for writing book reviews that you could try.
  – Write a letter to the author telling him how you feel about the book.
  – Produce a book review database on your computer.
  – Produce a book review for younger children.
  – Write a questionnaire about a book and ask others to complete it.
Use your imagination!

Stepping Stones to help you

• Title, author, publisher.
• My favourite character. Why? What did he/she do or say?
• The character I disliked. Why? What did he/she do or say?
• The story. My favourite part in the story. Why? Describe the episode.
• Anything I did not like? Describe the episode.
• Conclusion: why I like this book.
(Look at copymaster I.)

UNIT 20 Comparing Texts

Think ahead

We all know the story of 'Goldilocks and the Three Bears'. Here is a very different version. How is Roald Dahl's view of Goldilocks different from the usual one? Which version do you prefer?

Oh, what a tale of crime on crime!
Let's check it for a second time.

Crime One, the prosecution's case:
She breaks and enters someone's place.

Crime Two, the prosecutor notes:
She steals a bowl of porridge oats.

Crime Three: She breaks a precious chair
belonging to the Baby Bear.

Crime Four: She smears each spotless sheet
with filthy messes from her feet.

A judge would say without a blink,
"Ten years hard labour in the clink!"
But in the book, as you will see,
The little beast gets off scot-free,
While tiny children near and far
Shout, "Goody-good! Hooray! Hurrah!"
"Poor darling Goldilocks!" they say,
"Thank goodness that she got away!"
Myself, I think I'd rather send
Young Goldie to a sticky end.
"Oh daddy!" cried the Baby Bear,
"My porridge gone! It isn't fair!"
"Then go upstairs," the Big Bear said,
"Your porridge is upon the bed.
But as it's inside mademoiselle,
You'll have to eat her up as well."

'Goldilocks and the Three Bears'
from *Revolting Rhymes* by Roald Dahl

Thinking back

1 Roald Dahl has put Goldilocks on trial. Which words tell you this?
2 Write down what he sees as her four crimes.
3 What does the traditional fairy story of Goldilocks say about these four things?
4 Explain how Goldilocks gets off 'scot-free' in the original story.
5 How would Roald Dahl like the story to end?

Thinking about it

Think about the fairy tale version of Goldilocks. Copy and complete the chart to compare the traditional tale with Roald Dahl's version. Use copymaster 20 to help you.

Traditional fairy tale	Roald Dahl's version
Serious Goldilocks the heroine Bears the villains	

Write a few paragraphs. Use your notes. Compare the two versions.

Thinking it through

Write two versions of a traditional tale, for example 'Little Red Riding Hood' or 'The Three Little Pigs'.
– First tell the story as you would to a young child.
– Then tell a different version of the story, for example from the wolf's viewpoint. Does Little Red Riding Hood deserve to get eaten if she cannot tell her grandmother from a wolf? Are the three little pigs as innocent as they seem? Who are the real heroes and villains?
– You do not have to write it in verse.

Stepping Stones to help you

• In which places and times are the different texts set?
• What is the language of each text like?
• What kinds of texts are we dealing with? Serious? Funny? Historical?
• Who are the heroes and villains?
(See copymaster J for guidance.)

UNIT 21   Writing a Poem Sequence

Think ahead

Short poems which follow a pattern can be joined together to make a 'poem sequence'. Poems are patterns. Some rhyme; some do not. What pattern can you see in a haiku?

Syllable writing
Counting out your seventeen
Doesn't produce poem.

Good haiku need thought
One simple statement followed
By poet's comment.

The town dump is white
With seagulls, like butterflies
Over a garden.

From *Haiku* by David McCord

*Shiki, one of Japan's greatest haiku poets,
gave this advice about writing haiku:*

Remember perspective. Large things are large,
but small things are also large if seen close up.
Keep the words tight; put in nothing useless.
Cut down as much as possible on adverbs and verbs.
Use both imaginary pictures and real ones,
but prefer the real ones.

From *An Introduction to Haiku* by H G Henderson

Thinking back

1 How many syllables should there be in a haiku?
2 What else does this poet, David McCord, say is needed besides this pattern?
3 Write down the two ingredients from the second haiku that David McCord says a haiku should have.
4 Write out the third haiku. Label it with:
   – the number of syllables in each of the three lines;
   – the simple statement;
   – the poet's comment.

 Thinking about it

Write your own haiku for each season of the year. Describe the features of each season.
– Try to think of unusual comparisons to surprise your reader.
– Use copymaster 21 to help you plan your haiku.

 Thinking it through

Another interesting pattern is the 'cinquain'. It starts off with 2 syllables, goes on to 4, then 6, then 8 and then snaps back to 2.

    2 syllables → August,
    4 syllables → The beach is full,
    6 syllables → Burning crowds fry in oil,
    8 syllables → We submerge in the splashing waves,
    2 syllables → Heaven!

Write a series of four 'cinquain' describing parts of your school day.
Use the Stepping Stones to help you.

Stepping Stones to help you

• Decide what type of poem you want to write.
• Decide what pattern it will follow.
• Make rough notes of your ideas.
• Use your notes to make a first draft and change any ideas you want.
• Write a best copy.
(Use copymaster Q, Writing a Poem, to give you guidance.)

UNIT 22   Writing in Paragraphs

Think ahead

In this story from Trinidad, the writer tells us about an important episode in his childhood. If he had not written in paragraphs, how easy would this story have been to read and understand? We use paragraphs when we write about something different or when we write speech. Does the writer stick to these rules?

In the rainy season we got few chances to play cricket in the road. For whenever we were at the game, the rains came down, chasing us into the yard again. That was the way it was in Mayaro in the rainy season. The skies were always overcast, and over the sea the rain-clouds hung low and grey and scowling, and the winds blew in and whipped angrily through the palms. And when the winds were strongest and raging, the low-hanging clouds would become dense and black, and the sea would roar, and the torrents of rain would come sweeping with all their tumult upon us.

We had just run in from the rain. Amy and Vern from next door were in good spirits, and laughing, for oddly enough they seemed to enjoy the downpours as much as playing cricket in the road.

"Rain, rain, go to Spain," they shouted. And presently their mother, who must have heard the noise and knew, appeared from next door, and Vern and Amy vanished through the hedge.

I stood there, depressed about the rain, and then I put Vern's bat and ball underneath the house, and went indoors. I was sitting, sad, and wishing that the rain would really go away – go to Spain, as Vern said – when my heart seemed to jump out of me. A deafening peal of thunder struck across the sky. Quickly I closed the window. The rain hammered awfully on the roof-top, and I kept tense for the thunder which I knew would break again and for the unearthly flashes of lightning.

Secretly I was afraid of the violent weather. I was afraid of the rain, and of the thunder and the lightning that came with them, and of the sea beating against the headlands, and of the storm-winds, and of everything being so death-like when the rains were gone. I stared again at another flash of lightning and before I had recovered from this, yet another terrifying peal of thunder hit the air. I screamed. I heard my mother running into the room. Thunder struck again and I dashed under the bed.

"Selo! Selo! First bat!" Vern shouted from the road. The rains had ceased and the sun had come out, but I had not quite recovered yet. I brought myself reluctantly to look out from the front door, and there was Vern, grinning and impatient and beckoning me.

"First bat," he said. And as if noticing my indifference he looked towards Amy who was just coming out to play. "Who second bat?" he said.

"Me!" I said.

"Me!" shouted Amy almost at the same time.

"Amy second bat," Vern said.

"No, I said 'me' first," I protested.

Vern grew impatient while Amy and I argued. Then an idea seemed to strike him. He took out a penny from his pocket. "Toss for it," he said. "What you want?"

"Heads," I called.

"Tail," cried Amy, "tail bound to come!"

The coin went up in the air, fell down and overturned, showing tails.

"I'm not playing!" I cried, stung. And as that did not seem to disturb them enough, I ran towards where I had put Vern's bat and ball and disappeared with them behind our house. Then I flung them with all my strength into the bushes.

When I came back to the front of the house, Vern was standing there dumbfounded. "Selo, where's the bat and ball!"

I was fuming. "I don't know about any bat and ball!"

"Tell on him," Amy cried. "He throw them away."

Vern's mouth twisted into a forced smile. "What's an old bat and ball," he said.

But as he walked out the yard I saw tears glinting from the corners of his eyes.

For the rest of that rainy season we never played cricket in the road again.

From *Cricket in the Road* by Michael Anthony

Thinking back

1 Write down two details in the first paragraph that give you the idea that the story is set on a tropical island.
2 What is Selo afraid of?
3 Why is Selo in such a bad mood when he is asked to bat?
4 What does he do that causes the bad feeling among the friends?
5 Do you think his friends should have acted differently?

Thinking about it

1 Look at the story again. Go through it paragraph by paragraph and copy and complete the chart below to see how and when paragraphs are used.

Paragraph	Paragraph about
1	Why they could not play cricket often because of the bad weather.
2	Amy and Vern enjoying themselves in the rain. Selo not.

2 Continue the story in your own words. Write five more paragraphs.
Use copymaster 22 to help you plan your story.
Did his friends ever forgive Selo? How did they deal with him?
What did Selo do to make amends for his thoughtless act?

Thinking it through

Write a story about something you did when you were very young that you are now ashamed of. Remember to use paragraphs.
– In your story, try to describe how you thought as a child.
– Describe the effect of your actions on others around you. How did they feel? How did they react to your behaviour?

Stepping Stones to help you

- Spelling: check in a dictionary or use a spell check on your computer.
- Punctuation: have you written in sentences? used capital letters and full stops? punctuated speech correctly?
- Paragraphs: How will you set out your work in sections? Does each new idea have its own paragraph? Is speech set out correctly?

(Use copymaster K to help you edit your work.)